Learning LOL

Welcome to my class about the Winter Olympics! My name is Professor Charlie, and I am so excited to show you all the fun things my assistant and I have been learning. My assistant is my mom, and she is super helpful! She reads all of the research we do together out loud, takes me for walks when it is time for a break, finds yummy treats for the both of us to share, and also does all the typing since she has fingers and thumbs, and I only have paws, and the most important thing of all, she gives the best belly rubs. My job is to give her fun ideas to look up, to keep her warm with cuddles, and to try not to bark at the mailman. I make no promises about the last one. We make a really great team!

Next week, we are supposed to get a huge snowstorm in Michigan, which means going for walks might be hard, so my assistant and I decided to bundle up today and go to the park for a walk so I could run in the snow. I saw many people playing in the snow at the park. People were making snowmen, and others were having snowball fights. I was so excited for my assistant to make a snowball for me to run and catch. This is my favorite winter game. Don't worry! She always makes sure there is no yellow snow in my snowballs! After about an hour, my assistant started getting cold, so she said it was time to go. But I looked up at her, gave her the biggest puppy dog eyes, and asked her to please throw one more snowball. Of course, she said yes because my puppy dog eyes always work on her. She threw it so far this time, but I knew I could get it. I ran as fast as I could and jumped so high, and with all my might, I got it! After eating my snowball, I looked up and couldn't believe my eyes. I saw some people in the distance, and they looked like they were floating across the snow. I must have fallen asleep or hit my head because I don't think people can float unless my assistant has been keeping something from me! I ran back to my assistant and told her what I saw.

It took me a moment to calm down and catch my breath. I told her what I saw and asked her why she didn't tell me that she could float! She looked at me, a little confused because people don't float, so she asked me to show her the floating people. After a short walk on the snowy and icy path, I saw the people and pointed to them. As we continued walking

closer to the people, my mom, I mean, my assistant, giggled a little and told me that I was right and it looked like people were floating from far away. We stopped, and she bent down to my level and told me they were figure skating or ice skating on the ice. She suggested that we get closer so I could see what they were doing.

We found a bench beside a frozen pond and warmed up with hot apple cider that we had brought with us as we watched the people glide across the ice. I saw that they had special shoes with sharp blades on them that helped them glide across the ice. It was amazing to see all the spins and jumps they were doing. My assistant explained that figure skating is one of many kinds of winter sports. I had no idea you could play sports on the ice or in the snow. This was very exciting news, and my tail began to wag! She then told me that there was a very special sporting event that only happens every four years in the winter, and it is called the Winter Olympics. During these special games, women and men worldwide will challenge each other to see who is the best in their sport. I asked her if snowball chasing was an Olympic sport, but she sadly said no. So I asked her what were the other winter sports. She said we should go home, get warmed up, get a snack, and do some research.

After we got home, my assistant made us our favorite snack (peanut butter & apples), and I gently got my assistant's laptop for her and placed it on our cozy sofa. When we were all snuggled up under a blanket with our snack and computer, we looked up what sports were in the Winter Olympics. There were so many different events that I lost count. To be honest, I can only count to 20 because that's how many fingers and toes my assistant has. I am still learning my numbers. We learned that thousands and thousands of years ago, people were skiing and ice skating in their everyday lives, like traveling to their friend's homes and hunting for food. I can't believe there were no supermarkets or cars back then! Then, in France in 1924, the first Winter Olympics was, with only 14 different events. The Winter Olympics became so popular that over the years, more events were added; as of 2022, there were 109 different events. We also discovered that there were Summer Olympics, but that will be a different book.

I closed my eyes and thought about myself racing towards the finish line on my snowboard, with the wind and snow rushing past my ears, trying to beat the dog next to me. And I cross the finish line first, winning the gold medal or maybe a big, yummy dog bone. But then, I was sad to find out there were no Olympic games for dogs, but I could enter a thing called a "dog show." I will have to do some extra research about this kind of show, but I feel like I might have to go to the groomers. I hate taking baths! After we had finished learning about the different events and thinking about the cool sports I could try in the future, we decided to write this book for you, my pup pal! Please don't worry if you don't understand something that I wrote because I made sure everything was super easy to look up if you didn't understand. You can even find videos of each sport online. It was so fun watching each one! Looking up things you don't know is a wonderful way for you to learn how to be a researcher, like me! But please ask an adult if it is ok to use the computer before you begin your research. Manners and safety first! I hope you enjoy our book, our new pup pal. We will see you for your next lesson!

Tara & Charlie Morrish

Photos by
Scarlet Morr ish

Professor Charlie

Smokey

Learninglol.com

Learning LOL

Where learning language online is fun!

We want to thank you, from the bottom of our paws to the tips of our ears, for buying our book! We hope you enjoyed reading it as much as we enjoyed writing and researching it. We are also excited to share that you can join us on our website soon. Here, you can view your favorite topics with videos, maps, pictures, interactive worksheets, and flashcards. To make entering the classroom easier, scan the QR code, but remember to ask your grown-up before going online. See you there!

Have fun learning online!

Have fun learning with more books!

Where learning language online is fun!

Learning About Olympic Sports!

Table of Contents

The picture that couldn't be found during Olympic Events

Where learning language online is fun!

Learning About Olympic Sports!

Alpine Skiing or Ski Racing

History

🐰 Skiing was initially used for hunting and transportation from as early as 10,000 BC by people in Northern Asia and Europe. Archaeologists have found cave paintings and pieces of wooden skis dating back about 10,000 years. Later, soldiers used them in different parts of the military in these northern countries.

🐰 In later years in these countries, skis would be used by the military, farmers, and for hunting wild animals because it was the fastest kind of transportation. By the late 1800s, people were skiing for fun when competitions like cross-country skiing, downhill skiing, and ski jumping started.

Equipment Used

🐰 Skis, poles, binding (they hold the boot to the ski), goggles, helmets, racing suits, and sometimes racers will use wax on the bottoms of their skis to help them glide over the snow better.

❦ In the past, skis had a solid piece of wood like ash or hickory, but today, they are made out of a wooden core surrounded by fiberglass layers with titanium (metal) edges.

<u>Rules</u>

❦ Each event has its own set of rules. See below.

<u>11 events in this category</u>

❧ **<u>Women's & Men's Alpine Combined:</u>** Each person will have one turn on the Downhill and the Slalom. The athlete with the best-combined score will take a medal. **(Added to the Garmisch Partenkirchen (Germany) Winter Olympics in 1936)**

❧ **<u>Women's & Men's Slalom:</u>** Skiers race down the track through sets of poles or "gates." They do not have to hit the poles, but most do because it will give the skier the fastest and most direct path to the finish line. Skiers must make their way around each "gate," alternating around each one. Skiers can go as fast as 60-70 kph (37-44 mph). Skiers will have two runs, each on a different course. **(Added to the San Moritz (Switzerland) Winter Olympics in 1948)**

❧ **<u>Women's & Men's Downhill</u>:** Athletes will race down the track between 2.4-5 km (1.5-3 mi), going over hills and turns. Racers can reach speeds up to 129 kph (80 mph), if not faster, depending on the course and conditions. Each skier gets one run to get the best score. **(Added to the San Moritz (Switzerland) Winter Olympics in 1948)**

❧ **<u>Women's & Men's Giant Slalom:</u>** Skiiers must race down a track also going through poles or "gates," but on this course, the poles or "gates" are more spread out. Skiers must make their way around each "gate," alternating around each one. They can reach speeds of 80 kph (50 mph).

Each athlete will have two runs, each on a different course. **(Added to the Oslo (Norway) Winter Olympics in 1952)**

Women's & Men's Super G: Athletes go down a less steep downhill but with much tighter turns, and the course is not as wide. Racers can reach speeds up to 129 kph (80 mph), if not faster, depending on the track and conditions. Each athlete only gets one turn. **(Added to the Calgary (Canada) Winter Olympics in 1988)**

Mixed Team Event: This is a combination event for men and women, with two men and two women from each country on a team. They will compete in the parallel slalom, where athletes will race against each other down the slalom racecourse. After four heats, the team with the most wins will receive a medal. **(Added to the Pyeongchang (South Korea) Winter Olympics in 2018)**

Men's Giant Slalom Team Austria 2018 Pyeongchang

Men's Downhill 2018 Pyeongchang

Where learning language online is fun!

Learning About Olympic Sports!

Men's Super G 2010 Vancouver

Men's Slalom Team USA 2010 Vancouver

Skiing Parallel Slalom 2013 World Cup

Biathlon

History

❦ Skiing has been around northern European countries and Northern Asia for thousands of years. Archaeologists have found cave paintings and pieces of wooden skis dating back about 10,000 years.

❦ The biathlon was initially used for hunting in the northern Scandinavian countries as long ago as 4,000 years ago. The more modern version was in the 18th century when Northern Europe and Scandinavian countries held military competitions against each other. In 1924, a more familiar version was introduced as an army patrol. Biathlon was a demonstration event that included ski mountaineering, skiing, and rifle shooting. The demonstration events continued for the 1928, 1936, and 1948 Winter Olympics, then stopped until the 1960 Olympics, when we have our most current version of the sport.

Equipment Used

❦ Skis, poles, binding (they hold the boot to the ski), goggles, helmet, and racing suit. They also use a rifle (.22 caliber rifle) with magazines (it holds the bullets) with five bullets. They use a sling and harness to help keep the

rifle in place, as well as a scope, and a snow cover (it stops snow from getting into the rifle).

❆ In the past, skis had a solid piece of wood like ash or hickory, but now they have a wooden core surrounded by layers of fiberglass with titanium (a kind of metal) edges.

Rules

❆ In this sport, athletes combine cross-country skiing and rifle shooting.

❆ Each race will have 2-4 targets to shoot at from about 50 m (165 ft) away. Each athlete must stand or lie down to shoot their target, depending on the requirements of the target. If the shooter misses, time will be added to their final score, or they will have to ski extra laps (only during the sprint, pursuit, and mass start events).

11 events in this category

Women

🎯 **7.5 km Sprint, 10 km Pursuit, 12.5 km Mass Start, 15 km Individual, and 4X6 Relay** (Added the women's events to the Albertville (France) Winter Olympics in 1992)

Men

🎿 **10 km Sprint, 12.5 km Pursuit, 15 km Mass Start, 20 km individual, and 4 x 7.5 Relay** (Added to the Squaw Valley (USA) Winter Olympics in 1960)

Mixed Teams

🐾**Mixed Relay:** (men and women) **4 x 6 km. (Added to the Sochi (Russia) Winter Olympics in 2014)**

2010 Vancouver (Shooters Laying down)

Team USA 2010 Vancouver (Shooters Standing)

Women's Mass start 2022 Beijing

Shooting Target

Where learning language online is fun!

Learning About Olympic Sports!

Bobsledding

History

❦ There are early references to people using sledding for fun and sport around the 1400s in northern European countries. In the early 1880s, English soldiers stationed in Switzerland made a curved road (track) between two cities where they would use metal sleds and toboggans to get back and forth. They would use this to help transport supplies and to have fun. Soon after, people started using the metal sleds more for fun, and a few years later, it would become a major sporting event.

❦ Like the luge and skeleton, bobsledding was invented in Switzerland in the late 19th century when a steering mechanism was attached to a wooden toboggan. Some evidence might suggest that this sport was created in Albany, N.Y., a few years before the Swiss made it.

❦ The first bobsledding club was formed in St. Moritz, Switzerland, in 1897.

❦ They named this sport "Bobsledding" because people's heads "bob" back and forth to help gain more speed.

Equipment Used

❡ Sled, helmet, racing suit, and spiked shoes.

❡ Each team event will race down a 1,615 m (about 1 mi) track with multiple curves. The track has a different layout for every Olympics.

❡ The first bobsleds were very different from what they are today. They were two skeleton sleds, so they had no sides or covered front and were mostly made of wood and steel. Today, they are more like race cars, with the sides and front covered and made with fiberglass, a steel frame, and the most advanced aerospace technology.

Rules

❡ Teams have 1, 2, or 4 riders who slide down the track for the fastest time. Each team will have four runs to get their best time.

4 events in this category

🛷 **Women's Monobob**: Every athlete uses an identical sled with only one rider, the pilot. They use the same sled so the athletes can show their skills and not the technology of their bobsl ed. Each athlete will have four runs, and whoever has the fastest time after the four runs will win the gold. Racers can go as fast as 120 kph (75 mph) down the track. **(Added to the Beijing (China) Winter Olympics in 2022)**

🛷 **2 Women**: In this event, there are two riders, the pilot and the breakman. Racers can go as fast as 129 kph (80 mph). **(Added to the Salt Lake City (USA) Winter Olympics in 2002)**

🛷 **2 Men:** In this event, there are two riders, the pilot and the breakman. Racers can go as fast as 145 kph (90 mph). **(Added to the Lake Placid (USA) Winter Olympics in 1932)**

🛷 **4 Men:** In this event, four riders, a driver, two pushers, and a breakman. Racers can go as fast as 149 kph (93 mph). **(Added to the first official Winter Olympics in Chamonix (France) in 1924)**

Women's Monobob 2022 Beijing

2 Women Team USA 2014 Sochi

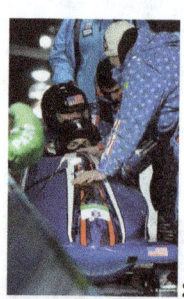

2 Men Team USA 2010 Vancouver

4 men Team Canada 2010 Vancouver

Learning LOL

Where learning language online is fun!

Learning About Olympic Sports!

Cross-country Skiing

History

❤ Skiing has been around northern European countries and Northern Asia for about 10,000 years. Archaeologists discovered cave paintings and ski pieces in parts of Russia and China dating back to this time. People from these regions also use skiing for transportation and fun.

❤ In later years in these countries, skis would be used by the military, farmers, and for hunting wild animals because it was the fastest kind of transportation. By the late 1800s, people were skiing for fun when competitions like cross-country skiing, downhill skiing, and ski jumping started.

Equipment Used

❤ Skis, poles, binding (they hold the boot to the ski), goggles, racing suits, and sometimes racers will use different kinds of waxes on the bottoms of their skis to help them glide over the snow better.

❤ In the past, skis had a solid piece of wood like ash or hickory, but now they have a wooden core surrounded by layers of fiberglass with titanium (a kind of metal) edges.

Rules

❦ Cross-country skis are different from alpine skis. They are longer, thinner, and lighter.

❦ There are two different types of ski styles that the athletes use: Freestyle (uses a side-to-side motion) & Classical (moves skis forward in parallel).

❦ **Classic**: Men and women will race individually only using the classical style, and the athlete with the fastest time wins. Each athlete only races one time.

❦ **Skiathlon**: Women and men race individually and will use both skiing styles. The athletes will start the race using the classical style, and then halfway through the race, they will change their skis and switch to freestyle skiing to finish the race. Each athlete only races one time.

❦ **Sprint**: Women and men race individually using only the freestyle ski style, and the fastest time wins. This event has multiple rounds, with the fastest times advancing. The men's track is 1.4 km (.87 mi) long and 1.2 km (.75 mi) for women.

❦ **Mass Start:** All women and all men athletes (during their category) will start the race together in the longest race of the cross country events. Athletes will race around a track instead of open country for this race. During the 2022 Olympics, athletes will use freestyle, but in the 2018 games, the racers will use the classical style. Each skier will only race once, and the fastest time wins.

❦ **Relay**: Men and women will race in a 4-person team, each racing part of the course using both skiing styles. The first two athletes will race in the classical style, and the last two will use the freestyle. Each team only races once.

12 events in this category

Women

🎿 **10 km Classic** (Added to the Oslo (Norway) Winter Olympics in 1952)

🎿 **7.5 km + 7.5 km Skiathlon** (Added to the Albertville (France) Winter Olympics in 1992)

🎿 **30 km Mass Start Free** (Added to the Sarajevo (Yugoslavia) Winter Olympics in 1984)

🎿 **Sprint Free** (Added to the Salt Lake City (USA) Winter Olympics in 2002)

🎿 **Team Sprint Classic** (Added to the Torino(Italy) Winter Olympics in 2006)

🎿 **4 x 5 Relay** (Added to the Cortina d'Ampezzo (Italy) Winter Olympics in 1956)

Men

🎿 **15 km Classic** (Added to the first official Winter Olympics in Chamonix (France) in 1924)

🎿 **15 km & 15 km Skiathlon** (Added to the Albertville (France) Winter Olympics in 1992)

🎿 **50 km Mass Start Free** (Added to the first official Winter Olympics in Chamonix (France) in 1924))

🎿 **Sprint Free** (Added to the Salt Lake City (USA) Winter Olympics in 2002)

Where learning language online is fun!

Learning About Olympic Sports!

🎿 **Team Sprint Classic** (Added to the Torino(Italy) Winter Olympics in 2006)

🎿 **4 x 10 Relay** (Added to the first official Winter Olympics in Garmisch-Partenkirchen in 1936)

Women's 4 x 5 Relay Team USA 2010 Vancouver (Handoff)

Women's Mass Start 2010 Vancouver

Men's Sprint Free Team ROC (both) 2010 Vancouver (Finish)

Men's 30 km Pursuit 2010 Vancouver

Curling

History

❦ The sport of curling is one of the oldest team sports. It began in Scotland in the 1500s. People would play on frozen lakes or lochs and use different rock materials from the regions of Perth and Stirling.

❦ In 1838, the first curling club was formed in Scotland, where they came up with the rules for the game. In 1842, Queen Victoria and Prince Albert visited the club, and Prince Albert loved it, so he made it one of his "patronages" (this means to help support the club), and it was renamed the "Royal Caledonian Curling Club" in 1843.

Equipment Used

❦ Curling stone, special shoes with one shoe that helps the athletes grip the ice, and the other allows them to slide, and a broom.

❦ Today, the curling stones are made from a rare granite found in only two places in the world, Scotland and Wales. This granite is very tough and absorbs little water. Each curling stone weighs 17- 20 kg (38-44 lbs).

Rules

❦ Each team is made up of 4 athletes (the mixed doubles only have two athletes, a man and a woman) who try and get their curling stone as close to the center "button" of the bullseye "house." The "house" at the end of the lane is a 46 m (150 ft) ice lane called a "sheet." Each team will throw eight stones.

❦ There are three players on the ice at one time. One person throws the stone down the "sheet" while the other two players are "sweeping" the ice to help the stone move where they want it to go. The 4th player is on reserve, but they all rotate through the positions and have particular jobs. The "Lead" throws the first two stones. "Second" throws the 3rd and 4th stones. "Third" throws the 5th and 6th stones. "Skip" throws the 7th and 8th stones.

❦ The tea with the most points at the end of 10 rounds wins and will advance to the next round.

3 events in this category

🥌 **Men's Curling:** The team has four men. **(Added to the first official Winter Olympics in Chamonix (France) in 1924, but then was made a demonstration sport (played only to promote the sport) until the Nagano (Japan) Winter Olympics in 1998 unit it was officially a part of the program)**

🥌 **Women's Curling:** The team is made up of 4 women. **(Added to the Nagano (Japan) Winter Olympics in 1998)**

🥌 **Mixed Doubles Curling:** The team has only one woman and one man. **(Added to the Pyeongchang (South Korea) Winter Olympics in 2018)**

Where learning language online is fun!

Learning About Olympic Sports!

Curling Stone, Broom, and Bullseye

Men's Team USA 2022 Beijing

Women's Team Sweden 2010 Vancouver (3 Sweepers)

Mixed Doubles Team ROC 2018 Pyeongchang

Where learning language online is fun!

Learning About Olympic Sports!

Figure Skating

History

❦ Ice skating was first used as a helpful way to travel during winter in Scandinavian countries as far back as 5,000 years ago. They used animal bones like cattle and horses and would attach them to the bottom of their feet.

❦ Figure skating became a trendy pastime for people in the years to come. Still, people at this time skated formally and usually very stiffly, with someone calling out different positions for the skater.

❦ In 1860, a man named Jackson Haines modernized the sport of figure skating by combining ballet moves and music to figure skating.

Equipment Used

❦ Ice rink, ice skates, performance costume with thick tights to keep the athlete's legs warm.

Rules

❦ Each event has its own set of rules. See below.

5 events in this category

Single events

🐾**Women Single Skate:** Each athlete must skate in a **"Short Program,"** about 2 min and 40 seconds long. Each performance must have some elements like spins, jumps, and footwork. Only the top-scoring skaters will advance to the **"Long Program."** The athlete's second program is about 4 minutes long and must show their technical skills. The skater with the highest total score from both performances will win. **(This event was added to the London (England) Summer Olympics in 1908, the 1920 Antwerp (Belgium) Summer Olympics, and then permanently added to the first official Winter Olympics in Chamonix (France) in 1924)**

🐾**Men Single Skate:** Each athlete must skate in a **"Short Program,"** about 2 min and 40 seconds long. Each performance must have a certain number of elements, like spins, jumps, and footwork. Only the top-scoring skaters will advance to the **"Long Program."** The athlete's second program is about 4 minutes and 30 seconds long, in which they must also show their technical skills. The skater with the highest total score from both performances will win. **(This event was added to the London (England) Summer Olympics in 1908, the 1920 Antwerp (Belgium) Summer Olympics, and then permanently added to the first official Winter Olympics in Chamonix (France) in 1924)**

3 events in this category

Mixed events

🐾 **Ice Dance:** This is a partner skate. It is made up of 2 events, **"Short Dance"** (about 2 minutes and 50 seconds long) and **"Free Dance"**

(about 4 minutes long). Skaters do not perform big tricks like jumps and flips in these events. It is more about spins, lifts, and being in sequence without being no more than two arm lengths apart. **(Added to the Innsbruck (Austria) Winter Olympics in 1976)**

🐾 **Pair Skating:** A pair of skaters must skate in a **"Short Program,"** about 2 min and 40 seconds long. Each must-have performance element like spins, throws, jumps, footwork, and more acrobatics. Only the top-scoring pairs will advance to the next round, the **"Long Program."** The pair's second program is about 4 minutes and 30 seconds long, in which they must also show their technical skills. The team with the highest total score from both performances will win. **(This event was added to the London (England) Summer Olympics in 1908, the 1920 Antwerp (Belgium) Summer Olympics, and then permanently added to the first official Winter Olympics in Chamonix (France) in 1924)**

🐾 **Team Event:** Each country chooses one athlete or pair for each event: Men Singles, Women's singles, Ice Dancing, and Pairs. Each event is scored like the individual events but with the four events' combined scores. The country with the highest score after all the events will be the winner. **(Add to the Sochi (Russia) Winter Olympics in 2014)**

Where learning language online is fun!

Learning About Olympic Sports!

Women Free Skate Team Japan 2010 Vancouver

Men Short Program Team Kazakhstan 2014 Sochi

Pairs Short Program Team China 2010 Vancouver

Freestyle Skiing

History

🐾 Skiing has existed for over 10,000 years and was first used for hunting and transportation. Archaeologists have found cave paintings and pieces of wooden skis dating back about 10,000 years. Over the years, skiing became fun for people in their free time and eventually became a sport in the Olympics.

🎖️ In later years in these countries, skis would be used by the military, farmers, and for hunting wild animals because it was the fastest kind of transportation. By the late 1800s, people were skiing for fun when competitions like cross-country skiing, downhill skiing, and ski jumping started.

🐾 Between the 1950s and the 1960s in the United States, there were many advancements in ski equipment, and skiers could do more complex tricks.

Equipment Used

🐾 Skis, poles, binding (they hold the boot to the ski), goggles, helmet, racing suit, extra padding, and colored knee patch for getting the judge's attention. These knee patches are only for some events.

❦ In the past, skis had a solid piece of wood like ash or hickory, but now they have a wooden core surrounded by layers of fiberglass with titanium (a kind of metal) edges.

Rules

❦ Each event has its own set of rules. See below.

13 events in this category

🎿 **Men's & Women's Aerials:** In this event, athletes will ski off a steep ramp and perform different flips and twists while soaring through the air. Athletes need to complete complicated tricks, take-offs, and landings. The athletes with the highest scores will advance to the next round. There are five rounds. The avenge jump is about 20 m (66 ft) into the air. **(First added as a demonstration sport in the Calgary (Canada) Winter Olympics in 1988, and the Albertville (France) Winter Olympics in 1992 became an official part of the Winter Olympics)**

🎿 **Men's & Women's Moguls:** In this event, athletes will ski over snow-covered mounds called "moguls" and then ski off two small ramps to perform flips and twists. Skiers score points on their technique, speed, and jumps. The course is about 235 m (770 ft) long, and each mound is 3.5 m (11.5 ft) apart. Skiers go about 30 kph (18 mph). **(First added as a demonstration sport in the Calgary (Canada) Winter Olympics in 1988, and the Albertville (France) Winter Olympics in 1992 became an official part of the Winter Olympics)**

🎿 **Men's & Women's Ski Cross:** In this event, athletes race against each other (4 skiers at a time) down the track and must go over large hills and tight turns. The top two skiers who cross the finish line first will advance to the next round. The final round will be when only four athletes are left, and whoever is the fastest wins. Skiers can reach speeds of about

97 kph (60 mph) and will race a length of about 1.2 km (.80 mi). **(Added to the Vancouver (Canada) Winter Olympics in 2010)**

Men's & Women's Halfpipe: In this event, athletes ski down a halfpipe structure (U-shaped walls) to propel themselves into the air to perform tricks. Skiers get points on their run's skill, difficulty, and style. Each athlete will have two runs to get their best time and advance to the next round. Athletes can ski three times during the final heat with their best score counting. The skier with the highest score wins. The track is about 183 m (600 ft) long, with an average jump height of 3.3-6.7 m (11-22 ft). **(Add to the Sochi (Russia) Winter Olympics in 2014)**

Men's & Women's Slopestyle: In this event, skiers ski down the track over ramps, on the edges of raised platforms, rails, and hills to perform jumps, flips, and other tricks. Skiers have two runs to get their best time, and the skiers with the highest score will advance to the final. In the last race, skiers will have three runs, and the athlete with the top score wins. The course is about 488 m (1,600 ft) long. **(Add to the Sochi (Russia) Winter Olympics in 2014)**

Men's & Women's Big Air: In this event, skiers ski down a steep hill and launch themselves off a ramp to perform flips, twists, and jumps. Athletes can reach heights of 47 m (155 ft) above the ground after leaving the ramp. Athletes have three runs to get their best score to advance to the final. The final skiers will have three runs down the hill to get their best score. The athlete with the top score wins. **(Added to the Beijing (China) Winter Olympics in 2022)**

Aerials Mixed Team: Each team has three skiers, combining men and women. Each teammate will ski off a steep ramp and perform different flips and twists while soaring through the air. The three scores are combined, and the top teams will advance to the next round. Each teammate will have one run during the final, and their scores will again be

totaled together. The team with the highest score wins. The avenge jump is about 20 m (66 ft) into the air. **(Added to the Beijing (China) Winter Olympics in 2022)**

Men's Aerials Team China 2010 Vancouver

Women's Moguls Team France 2010 Vancouver

Men's Ski Cross Team's Switzerland, France, Canada, & New Zealand 2018 Pyeongchang

Women's Halfpipe Team Canada 2018 Pyeongchang

Where learning language online is fun!

Learning About Olympic Sports!

Men's Slopestyle Team USA 2014 Sochi

Women's Big Air Team Sweden 2022 Beijing

Learning About Olympic Sports!

Ice Hockey

History

❦ Ice skating was first used as a helpful way to travel during winter in Scandinavian countries as far back as 5,000 years ago. They used animal bones like cattle and horses and would attach them to the bottom of their feet.

❦ Different forms of "ball & stick" games have been played for hundreds if not thousands of years, but the modern indoor game of hockey started in the 1870s in Canada. Even the famous scientist Charles Darwin recorded a version of this game in the 1850s.

Equipment Used

❦ Ice rink, goal net, hockey-style ice skates, helmets, face mask, mouth guard, full-body pads, protective gloves, puck, and hockey sticks.

❦ A unique rubber makeup hockey puck, but the first outdoor pucks were frozen cow poop. People made other versions out of wood or stone.

❦ Pucks are frozen before each game between -10 and -6.7 C (14-20 f).

❦ The first hockey sticks were hand-carved from one piece of wood, usually from hornbeam or birch trees. Around the 1920s, 2 part sticks

gained popularity but were still made all from wood. In the 1950s, people started wrapping the blades in fiberglass, and by the early 1990s, people made the whole hockey stick from carbon fiber.

❌ The first hockey sticks had a flat blade, but in the 1960s, Chicago Blackhawks, Stan Mikita (a famous player) developed a curved blade. Today, this is the standard hockey stick all players use. Some claim that in the 1940s, someone else created the curved edge.

Rules

❌ This is a team sport. There are six players on the ice at one time, one being the goalie. Each team will try to get the "puck" into the net by skating on the ice using their hockey sticks to hit the puck into the net. There are three periods in each game, each lasting 20 minutes. The team with the most goals at the end of the game wins.

2 events in this category

🏒 **Men**: 25 men make up this team, but only six play at once. No professional NHL hockey players are usually on the team, but all athletes have played in college or other leagues. Playing for a college leaves a chance for more amateur players to play. **(added to the 1920 Antwerp (Belgium) Summer Olympics and then permanently added to the first official Winter Olympics in Chamonix (France) in 1924)**

🏒 **Women**: 23 women make up this team, but only six play at one time. No professional NHL hockey players are usually on the team, but all athletes have played in college or other leagues. Having no NHL leaves a chance for more amateur players to play. **(Added to the Nagano (Japan) Winter Olympics in 1998)**

Learning About Olympic Sports!

Men's Team USA & Norway 2010 Vancouver

Men's Team Canada 2010 Vancouver

Women's Team Canada 2014 Sochi

Women's Team USA & Sweden 2010 Vancouver

Where learning language online is fun!

Learning About Olympic Sports!

Luge

History

🐾 Sleds have been around for thousands of years. They have been found in the cold Scandinavian countries and the warm sands of Egypt as far back as 4,000 years. They were used as tools at first to help move things from place to place.

🐾 There are early references to people using sledding for fun and sport around the 1400s in northern European countries. In the early 1880s, English soldiers stationed in Switzerland made a curved road (track) between two cities where they would use metal sleds to get back and forth. They would use this to help transport supplies and to have fun. Soon after, people started using the metal sleds more for fun, and a few years later, it would become a major sporting event.

🐾 In the late 1880s in St. Mortiz, Switzerland, along with the sports bobsledding and skeleton, luge became a major sport. People from all over Europe came to compete and watch these sports.

Equipment Used

❦ Ice-covered track, sled, racing suit, helmet, gloves with spikes, face shield, a neck strap (it helps the rider's neck against high speeds), and boots.

❦ Wood made the first sleds with modern technology, plastic, metal, and carbon fiber.

❦ The track is about 1,615 m (about 1 mi) with multiple curves. The track has a different layout for every Olympics.

Rules

❦ Althletes race down the track on their sleds for the fastest time. Each team will have four runs to get their best time.

❦ Athletes go about 129- 145 kph (80-90 mph).

4 events in this category

🛷 **Men's Singles:** Each athlete will race down the track lying on top of a flat sled on their back. Each racer will have four runs, and judges will add each time together. The athlete with the highest score after their runs will be the winner. **(Added to the Innsbruck (Austria) Winter Olympics in 1964)**

🛷 **Doubles**: A pair of athletes (one athlete lays on top of the other) will race down twice. After their races, the judges will add up their times, and the team with the fastest time wins. **(Added to the Innsbruck (Austria) Winter Olympics in 1964)**

🛷 **Women's Singles**: Each athlete will race down the track lying on top of a flat sled on their back. Each racer will have four runs, and the judges

will add each time together. The athlete with the highest score after their runs will be the winner. **(Added to the Innsbruck (Austria) Winter Olympics in 1964)**

🛷 **Team Relay**: In this event, each of the three events will combine into one race: the women's singles, men's singles, and doubles. Women start the race, and after she touches the hanging sensor at the end of the track (this signals the next racer), the men's single racer will race down the track. After he touches the sensor, the doubles will take off down the track. The time with the fastest time will win. **(Added to the Sochi (Russia) Winter Olympics in 2014)**

Men's Singles Team Italy 2018 Pyeongchang

Men's Doubles Team South Korea 2018 Pyeongchang

Women's Singles Team USA 2010 Vancouver

Team Relay 2016 World Cup (Uses the same target as the Olympics)

Where learning language online is fun!

Learning About Olympic Sports!

Nordic Combined

History

🐾 People have been using skis for over 10,000 years to help them travel from place to place and to help them hunt. The people living in northern Europe, Russia, and Asia were the first to use this technology. Archaeologists have found cave paintings and pieces of wooden skis dating back about 10,000 years. In later years, people started using skis for more recreational uses.

🐾 In the early 1800s in Norway, Lieutenant Olaf Rye launched himself off a ramp on skis to perform the first-ever ski jump. He wanted to show his fellow soldiers how brave he was and flew about 9 m (30 ft).

🐾 In later years in these countries, skis would be used by the military, farmers, and for hunting wild animals because it was the fastest kind of transportation. By the late 1800s, people were skiing for fun when competitions like cross-country skiing, downhill skiing, and ski jumping started.

🐾 The original event was a normal hill with a cross-country distance of 18 km (11 mi). **(Added to the first official Winter Olympics in Chamonix (France) in 1924)**

Where learning language online is fun!

Learning About Olympic Sports!

<u>Equipment Used</u>

❤ Skis, poles, binding (they hold the boot to the ski), goggles, helmet, racing suit, and gloves.

❤ In the past, skis had a solid piece of wood like ash or hickory, but now they have a wooden core surrounded by layers of fiberglass with titanium (a kind of metal) edges.

<u>Rules</u>

❤ The Nordic combined comprises two events: Ski jumping & Cross country. Ski Jumpers jump first in this event, then cross-country skiers ski. Judges will then convert the total points for the jumper into time penalties for the cross-country event for the starting position. The word "Gundersen" refers to the method used to determine the order in which athletes start in the 2nd event, the cross-country portion.

<u>3 events in this category</u>

🎿 **<u>Men's Individual Gundersen normal hill/10 km</u>:** The normal hill is 98 m (322 ft) that athletes must jump from, and after all the jumpers complete their jumps, they will begin the 10 km (6.2 mi) cross-country event. **(Added to the Vancouver (Canada) Winter Olympics in 2010)**

🎿 **<u>Men's Individual Gundersen large hill/10 km</u>:** The large hill is 125 m (410 ft) that athletes must jump from, and after all the jumpers complete their jumps, they will begin the 10 km (6.2 mi) cross-country event. **(Added to the Vancouver (Canada) Winter Olympics in 2010)**

Men's Team Gundersen large hill/4 x 5 km: This is a team event of 4 athletes, in which each member will have one jump and will ski a portion in the cross-country event. The large hill is 125 m (410 ft) that athletes must jump, and after all of the jumpers are done with their jumps, they will begin their 5 km (3.1 mi) part of the cross-country event. **(Added to the Nagano (Japan) Winter Olympics in 1998)**

Ski Jumping Hill 2010 Vancouver

Men's 10 km Portion Team USA & France 2010 Vancouver

Ski Jump portion 2010 Vancouver

Where learning language online is fun!

Learning About Olympic Sports!

Skeleton

History

🐶 Sleds have been around for thousands of years. They have been found in cold Scandinavian countries and the warm sands of Egypt as far back as 4,000 years ago. They first used sleds to help move things from place to place.

🐶 In the early 1880s, English soldiers stationed in Switzerland made a curved road (track) between two cities where they would use metal sleds to get back and forth. They would use this to help transport supplies and to have fun. Soon after, people started using the metal sleds more for fun, and a few years later, it would become a major sporting event.

🐶 In the late 1880s, in St. Mortiz, Switzerland, a famous track called "outdoor enthusiasts built Cresta Run." This track attracted athletes from all over Europe, including bobsledding and luge. A few years later, the new sport of skeleton became a major sport with significant competition.

🐶 In 1892, an Englishman named Mr. Child made a new metal sled that some said looked like a skeleton. The new sled and, shortly after, the sport was called "skeleton." Riders lay on their stomach, their head at the front of the sleds, then move down the track to the finish line.

Equipment Used

❦ Sled, helmet, spiked boots, and gloves.

❦ The sleds are made of steel and fiberglass with two blades on the bottom and can go about 129-145 kph (80-90 mph).

❦ They are about 79-119 cm (31-47 in) long and about 46 cm (18 in) wide.

❦ The track is about 1,615 m (1 mi) with multiple curves. The track has a different layout for every Olympics.

Rules

❦ Each athlete gets four runs (takes four turns) down the track, and after all of the runs are completed, the judges will add up their times. The athlete with the fastest time wins.

2 events in this category

🛷 **Women's event**: **(Added to the Salt Lake City, (USA) Olympics in 2002)**

🛷 **Men's event:** **(Added to the Olympics for the years 1928 in St. Moritz (Switzerland) & 1948 in San Moritz (Switzerland) and was permanently added in 2002 at the Salt Lake City (USA) Winter Olympics)**

Where learning language online is fun!

Learning About Olympic Sports!

Women's Event Team Russia's Olympic Committee (ROC) 2022 Beijing (Push Start)

Men's Event Team Ireland 2010 Vancouver

Where learning language online is fun!

Learning About Olympic Sports!

Ski Jumping

History

❦ Skiing was initially used for hunting and transportation from as early as 10,000 BC by people in Northern Asia and Europe. Archaeologists have found cave paintings and pieces of wooden skis dating back about 10,000 years.

❦ The sport of Ski jumping started around 1808 in Norway when Lieutenant Olaf Rye launched himself off a ramp on skis to perform the first-ever ski jump. He did this in front of his fellow soldiers with strength and bravery. He jumped about 9.5 m (31 ft).

❦ In later years in these countries, skis would be used by the military, farmers, and for hunting wild animals because it was the fastest kind of transportation. By the late 1800s, people were skiing for fun when competitions like cross-country skiing, downhill skiing, and ski jumping started.

Equipment Used

❦ Skis, binding (they hold the boot to the ski), goggles, gloves, helmet, and racing suit.

❧ In the past, skis had a solid piece of wood like ash or hickory, but now they have a wooden core surrounded by layers of fiberglass with titanium (a kind of metal) edges.

❧ Over the years, with advancements in skiing equipment and ramps, skiers can now soar about 90-100 m (300-350 ft) with one jump.

Rules

❧ They score points on their landings, style, and distance. Each jumper will have two jumps, and those with the best-combined score will advance to the next round.

❧ Each athlete is about 6-8 m (20-26 ft) above the ground at their highest part of the jump, with an average speed of 96 kph (60 mph).

❧ Some of the events have different rules. See below for more details.

<u>5 events in this category</u>

❧ <u>**Men's Normal Hill Individual:**</u> Each athlete must ski down a ramp and fly down a steep hill past the 90 m (about 296 ft) K- point (where the mountain starts to flatten out). The farther from the K-point, the more points a skier will receive. **(Added to the Innsbruck (Austria) Winter Olympics in 1964)**

❧ <u>**Men's Large Hill Individual:**</u> Each athlete must ski down a ramp and fly down a steeper hill past the 120 m (about 394 ft), K-point (where the mountain starts to flatten). The farther from the K-point, the more points a skier will receive. **(Added to the first official Winter Olympics in Chamonix (France) in 1924)**

❧ <u>**Men's Large Hill Team:**</u> There are four men per team, and each skier has two runs. The teammate's times are combined, and the team with

the highest score will advance. **(Added to the Calgary (Canada) Winter Olympics in 1988)**

⛷ **Women's Normal Hill Individual:** Each athlete must ski down a ramp and fly down a steep hill past the 90 m (about 296 ft), K-point (where the mountain starts to flatten out). The farther from the K-point, the more points a skier will receive. **(Added to the Sochi (Russia) Winter Olympics in 2014)**

⛷ **Mixed Team Normal Hill:** Each team will have two men and two women who must ski down a ramp and fly down a steep hill past the 90 m (about 296 ft), K-point (the point where the hill starts to flatten out). Each skier gets to have two runs, and all scores will be added together, with the top score advancing to the next round. **(Added to the Beijing (China) Winter Olympics in 2022)**

Men's Event Team Japan 2018 Pyeongchang

Women's Event Team USA 2014 Sochi

Where learning language online is fun!

Learning About Olympic Sports!

Snowboarding

History

❦ There are a few countries that claim to have invented the snowboard. Some say it began in Eastern Europe over 150 years ago, and others say it was invented in America about 115 years ago. The most widely accepted place of creation is in America.

❦ Many people have said that they invented the snowboard, but the first person to patent the first snowboard was Vern Wicklun in 1917. When he was 13 years old, he made a snowboard out of wood around his house. He called it the "Bunker" and made it out of solid white oak, and in 1939 he patented it. At the time, it did not sell very well.

❦ In 1965, Sherman Poppen redesigned the "Bunker" and made the "Snurfer." It was made of maple wood and had a string attached to the front to help with steering and balance. He patented his board in 1966, and he sold millions of them.

❦ The modern snowboard was invented in the late 1970s by Jake Burton Carpenter, who coined the term "snowboard." Carpenter made his boards out of laminate maple wood, but today, they are made with a combination of fiberglass, wood, steel, and plastic.

❧ By the 1980s, snowboarding had taken off as a fun sport, but skiers were getting upset at the ski resorts where these snowboarders were riding. They claimed that snowboarders were putting skiers in danger with the way they rode down the slopes, and snowboarding was rude, didn't follow the rules, and didn't fit the style of the resorts.

❧ In the 1990s, snowboarding was widely accepted, and athletes used a snow halfpipe to perform aerial tricks and jumps.

Equipment Used

❧ Snowboard, boots, helmet, binding (it holds the boot to the snowboard), and goggles.

Rules

❧ Each event has its own rules. See below.

11 events in this category

Men and Women's Slopestyle: In this event, snowboarders go down the track over ramps, on the edges of raised platforms, rails, and hills, to perform jumps, flips, and other tricks and will be judged and scored based on their skills. Snowboarders have two runs to get their best time, and the snowboarder with the highest score will advance to the final. In the last event, snowboarders will have three runs, and the athlete with the top score wins. The course is about 488 m (1,600 ft) long. **(Added to the Sochi (Russia) Winter Olympics in 2014)**

Men and Women's Parallel Giant Slalom: Two snowboarders race against the clock (not each other) down a track while also going through poles or "gates," but on this course, the poles or "gates" are more spread out. Snowboarders must make their way around each "gate,"

alternating around each one. They can reach speeds of 70 kph (43 mph). There are two lanes, one red and one blue, and each athlete will have two runs, one on each course. The athlete's scores from each run are combined, and the snowboarders with the fastest scores will advance to the final round. During the last run, the athlete with the highest score or the two snowboarders racing can choose which lane to race on. The racer with the fastest time wins. **(Added to the Nagano (Japan) Winter Olympics in 1998)**

Women and Men's Snowboard Cross: In this event, athletes race against each other (6 snowboarders at a time) down the track and must go over large hills and tight turns. The top two snowboarders who cross the finish line first will advance to the next round. The final round will be when only four athletes are left, and whoever is the fastest wins. Snowboarders can reach speeds of about 97 kph (60 mph) and will race a length of about 1.2 km (.80 mi). **(Added to the Turin (Italy) Winter Olympics in 2006)**

Women and Men's Halfpipe: In this event, athletes snowboard down a halfpipe structure (U-shaped walls) to propel themselves into the air to perform tricks. Snowboarders score points on their run's skill, difficulty, and style. Each athlete will have two runs to get their best time and advance to the next round. During the final match, athletes will get to snowboard three times with their best score counting. The snowboarder with the highest score wins. The track is about 183 m (600 ft) long, with an average jump height of 3.3-6.7 m (11-22 ft). **(Added to the Nagano (Japan) Winter Olympics in 1998)**

Women and Men's Big Air: In this event, snowboarders go down a steep hill and launch themselves off a ramp to perform flips, twists, and jumps. Each snowboarder only gets to jump one time to get their best score. Athletes have two runs to get their best score to advance to the final.

Snowboarders will have three runs down the hill during their last run to get their best score, combining their top two scores. The athlete with the highest score wins. Athletes can reach heights of 47 m (155 ft) above the ground after leaving the ramp. **(Added to the Pyeongchang (South Korea) Winter Olympics in 2018)**

Mixed Team Snowboard Cross: In this event, teams are made of 1 man and one woman. The men race first, and then the women race next. They must race against each other down the track and must go over large hills and tight turns. The top two snowboarding teams who cross the finish line with the fastest combined score will advance to the next round. The final round will be when only four teams are left, and whoever has the quickest combined score wins. Snowboarders can reach speeds of about 97 kph (60 mph) and will race a length of about 1.2 km (.80 mi). **(Added to the Beijing (China) Winter Olympics in 2022)**

Men's Slopestyle Event Team USA 2018 Pyeongchang

Men's Parallel Gaint Slalom Team South Korea & Austria 2018 Pyeongchang

Where learning language online is fun!

Learning About Olympic Sports!

Women's Snowboard Cross Team's France (2 Boarder), Italy, & Australia 2018 Pyeongchang

Men's Halfpipe Team USA 2014 Sochi

Snowboarding Big Air Ramp 2018 Pyeongchang

Where learning language online is fun!

Learning About Olympic Sports!

Speed Skating

History

🐶 Ice skating was first used as a valuable way to travel during winter in Scandinavian countries as far back as 5,000 years ago. They used animal bones like cattle and horses and would attach them to the bottom of their feet.

🐶 Around the 1600s, speed skating gained popularity in cold northern European countries like the Netherlands and Scandinavia because of the new advances in the blades of the skates.

🐶 By the late 1800s, there were many speed skating clubs across Europe and America, and countries were holding World Championships to bring these countries together.

Equipment Used

🐶 Ice rink with lanes, speed ice skates, racing suit, gloves, helmet, and goggles.

🐶 Long track ice skate blades are 40-48 cm (16-19 in) long, with a slightly curved blade attached by a unique hinging device. This blade also detaches from the heel of the book when the skater is in motion. This device lets the

blade be on the ice longer, and the skater will go faster. These skates are "Clap skates."

❅ The "Clap skate" was developed in the early 1980s and was first used in the 1998 Olympics.

❅ Short-track ice skate blades are 30-45 cm (12-18 in) long.

<u>Short Track Speed Skating- 9 events in this category</u>

<u>Rules</u>

❅ The short track is an oval-shaped track that is about 111 m (365 ft) long. In every heat, 4-6 athletes will race against each other counter-clockwise around the track. Racers will move around each other and race around tight corners. The skaters with the fastest times will advance to the next round. The skater who has the quickest time after all the matches is the winner.

❅ This race takes speed, skill, and good start placement.

❅ They can go about 48 kph (30 mph), and athletes wear helmets.

<u>Women</u>

🐾 **500 m:** (4 ½ laps around the track) **(Added to the Albertville (France) Winter Olympics in 1992)**

🐾 **1000 m:** (9 laps around the track) **(Added to the Lillehammer (Norway) Winter Olympics in 1994)**

🐾 **1500 m:** (13 ½ laps around the track) **(Added to the St Lake City (USA) Winter Olympics in 2002)**

🐾 **3000 m Team Relay:** (This team has four women who each skate a portion of the 27 laps around the track) **(Added to the Albertville (France) Winter Olympics in 1992)**

Men

🐾 **500 m:** (4 ½ laps around the track) **(Added to the Lillehammer (Norway) Winter Olympics in 1994)**

🐾 **1000 m:** (9 laps around the track) **(Added to the Albertville (France) Winter Olympics in 1992)**

🐾 **1500 m:** (13 ½ laps around the track) **(Added to the St Lake City (USA) Winter Olympics in 2002**

🐾 **5000 m Team Relay:** (This team has four men who each skate a portion of the 45 laps around the track) **(Added to the Albertville (France) Winter Olympics in 1992)**

Mixed Teams

🐾 **Mixed Team 2000 m:** (18 laps around the track) Two men and two women from each country will skate. Each athlete will skate twice in this race. **(Added to the Beijing (China) Winter Olympics in 2022)**

Speed Skating (Long Track) 14 events in this category

Rules

🐕 The long track is a 400 m (1,312 ft) oval-shaped track. In this event, only two athletes are racing clockwise at a time, racing each other for the fastest time and against the times in the other heats. The skater with the

fastest overall time is the winner. That means that each skater will only race one time.

🐾 Skaters can go as fast or faster than 56 kph (35 mph) and do not wear helmets.

<u>Women</u>

(Was a demonstration sport in 1932 in the Lake Placid (USA) Winter Olympics)

🐾 **2x500 m:** (1 ¼ laps around the track) **(Added to the Squaw Valley (USA) Winter Olympics in 1960)**

🐾 **1000 m:** (2 ½ laps around the track)**(Added to the Squaw Valley (USA) Winter Olympics in 1960)**

🐾 **1500 m:** (3 ¾ laps around the track)**(Added to the Squaw Valley (USA) Winter Olympics in 1960)**

🐾 **3000 m:** (7 ½ laps around the track) **(Added to the Squaw Valley (USA) Winter Olympics in 1960)**

🐾 **5000 m:** (12 ½ laps around the track) **(Added to the Calgary (Canada) Winter Olympics in 1988)**

🐾 **Team pursuit:** (8 laps around the track) In this event, three skaters will take turns skating 2,400m (about 1.5 mi). Two teams will start the race on opposite sides straightaway in this race. The winner of the heat will move on to the next round. After all the runs, the team with the fastest time will win. **(Added to the Turin (Italy) Winter Olympics in 2006)**

🐾 **Mass start:** (16 laps around the track) In this event, all racers (max 24 skaters and all individual racers) will start the race together. This event

is won by "Sprint points," athletes can earn during their 4th, 8th, 12th, and 16th laps. Then, the points are added, and the skater with the most points wins. For example, if an athlete finishes the race in 4th place, but after the points are combined, this racer could win a medal. **(Added to the Pyeongchang (South Korea) Winter Olympics in 2018)**

<u>Men</u>

⛸ **2x500 m:** (1 ¼ laps around the track) **(Added to the first official Winter Olympics in Chamonix (France) in 1924)**

⛸ **1000 m** (2 ½ laps around the track) **(Added to the Innsbruck (Austria) in 1976)**

⛸ **1500 m** (3 ¾ laps around the track) **(Added to the first official Winter Olympics in Chamonix (France) in 1924)**

⛸ **5000 m** (12 ½ laps around the track) **(Added to the first official Winter Olympics in Chamonix (France) in 1924)**

⛸ **10,000 m:** (25 laps around the track) **(Added to the first official Winter Olympics in Chamonix (France) in 1924)**

<u>Mixed Teams</u>

⛸ **Team pursuit:** (8 laps around the track) In this event, a team of 3 skaters will take turns skating 3,200 m (about 2 mi). Two teams will start the race on opposite sides straightaway in this race. The winner of the heat will move on to the next round. After all the matches, the team with the fastest time will win. **(Added to the Turin (Italy) Winter Olympics in 2006)**

⛸ **Mass start:** (16 laps around the track) All racers (max 24 skaters) will start the race together in this event. They will skate 16 laps. This event is

won by "Sprint points," which athletes can earn during their 4th, 8th, 12th, and 16th lap. Then, the points are added, and the skater with the most points wins. For example, if an athlete finishes the race in 4th place, but after the points are totaled, this racer could win a medal. **(Added to the Pyeongchang (South Korea) Winter Olympics in 2018)**

Women's 3,000 m Team Japan 2010 Vancouver

(start)

Women's Relay Team's China & Poland 2010 Vancouver

Men's Mass Start 2018 Pyeongchang

Women's Team Pursuit Team Netherlands 2010 Vancouver

Equipment Then and Now

Early Ice Skate Made From Animal Bone

Different styles of snowboards

Snurfers

Where learning language online is fun!

Learning About Olympic Sports!

Example of an early sled

Early Bobsleds

Modern Bobsled

Early Skis

Modern Skis

Where learning language online is fun!

Learning About Olympic Sports!

Biathlon.22 rifle

Speed Skating Clap Skates

Speed Skates Short Track

Speed Skates Long Track

Men's Figure Skates

Where learning language online is fun!

Learning About Olympic Sports!

Women's Figure Skates

Hockey Skates

Hockey Puck

Where learning language online is fun!

Learning About Olympic Sports!

Don't forget to check out our other books, Daily Vocabulary Worksheets Volume 1 and 2 & Daily Vocabulary Flashcards Volume 1 and 2.

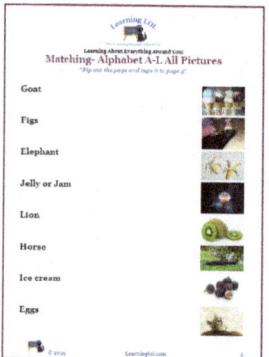

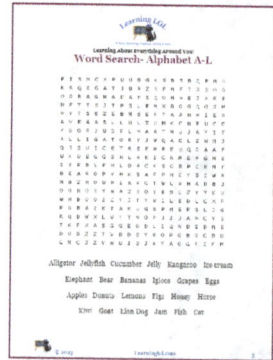

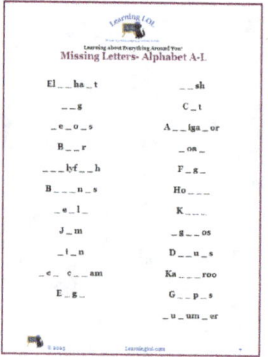

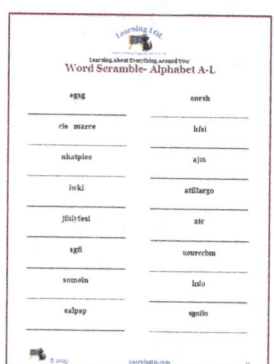

Where learning language online is fun!

Learning About Olympic Sports!

Learning About Olympic Sports!

Where learning language online is fun!

Learning About Olympic Sports!

Where learning language online is fun!

Learning About Olympic Sports!